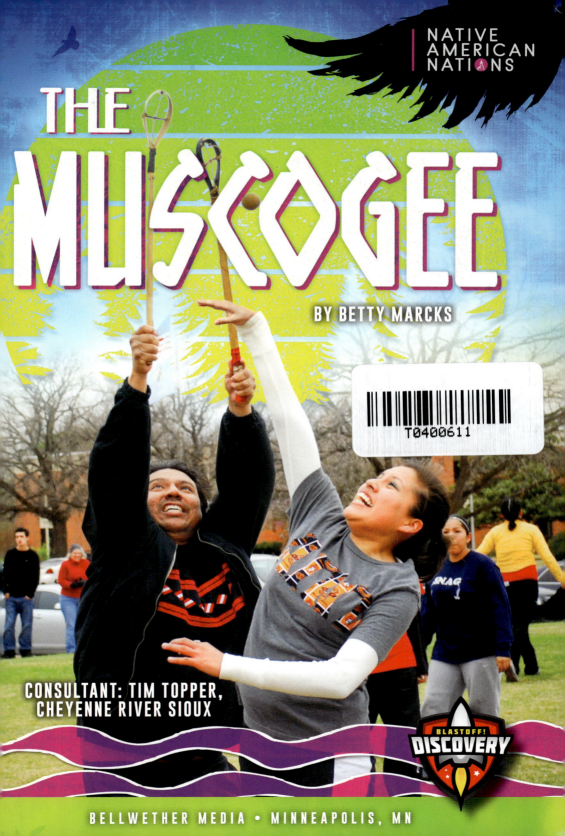

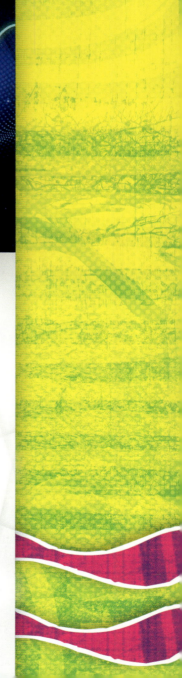

Author's Statement of Positionality:
I am a white woman of European descent. As such, I can claim no direct lived experience of being a Native American. In writing this book, I have tried to be an ally by relying on sources by Native American writers and authors whenever possible and have worked to let their voices guide its content.

This edition first published in 2025 by Bellwether Media, Inc.

No part of this publication may be reproduced in whole or in part without written permission of the publisher. For information regarding permission, write to Bellwether Media, Inc.,
Attention: Permissions Department,
6012 Blue Circle Drive, Minnetonka, MN 55343.

Library of Congress Cataloging-in-Publication Data

Names: Marcks, Betty, author.
Title: The Muscogee / by Betty Marcks
Description: Minneapolis, MN : Bellwether Media, Inc., 2025. | Series: Blastoff!
  discovery: Native American nations | Includes bibliographical references and index.
  | Audience: Ages 7-13 | Audience: Grades 4-6 | Summary: "Engaging images
  accompany information about the Muscogee people. The combination of high-interest
  subject matter and narrative text is intended for students in grades 3 through 8"
  – Provided by publisher.
Identifiers: LCCN 2024016021 (print) | LCCN 2024016022 (ebook) | ISBN
  9798893040074 (library binding) | ISBN 9798893041491 (paperback) |
  ISBN 9781644879399 (ebook)
Subjects: LCSH: Creek Indians–Juvenile literature.
Classification: LCC E99.C9 M39 2025 (print) | LCC E99.C9 (ebook) |
  DDC 975.004/97385–dc23/eng/20240513
LC record available at https://lccn.loc.gov/2024016021
LC ebook record available at https://lccn.loc.gov/2024016022

Text copyright © 2025 by Bellwether Media, Inc. BLASTOFF! DISCOVERY and associated logos are trademarks and/or registered trademarks of Bellwether Media, Inc. Bellwether Media is a division of Chrysalis Education Group.

Editor: Elizabeth Neuenfeldt   Series Designer: Andrea Schneider
Book Designer: Laura Sowers

Printed in the United States of America, North Mankato, MN.

TABLE OF CONTENTS

THE MVSKOKE	4
TRADITIONAL MUSCOGEE LIFE	6
EUROPEAN CONTACT	12
LIFE TODAY	16
CONTINUING TRADITIONS	20
FIGHT TODAY, BRIGHT TOMORROW	26
TIMELINE	28
GLOSSARY	30
TO LEARN MORE	31
INDEX	32

THE MVSKOKE

The Muscogee are peoples from a large Native American nation. Their name is **traditionally** spelled Mvskoke. Their homeland spans the Southeastern woodlands of the United States. It includes parts of today's Alabama, Georgia, and Florida. Their language is also named Mvskoke. It is a similar language to those of the Chickasaw, Choctaw, Alabama, and other nations who lived in the area.

A story recalls **ancestral** Muscogee being led east from western mountains. The Creator gave them a cedar pole. Each day, the people set up the pole and followed in the direction it fell. When the pole stayed standing, they had reached their home.

CHEAHA MOUNTAIN, MEANING "HIGH PLACE" IN MVSKOKE

TRADITIONAL MUSCOGEE LIFE

MISSISSIPPIAN EARTH MOUND AT ETOWAH INDIAN MOUNDS STATE HISTORIC SITE

Muscogee peoples are the **descendants** of the **Mississippian Culture**. Mississippian people arrived near the Ocmulgee River around 900 CE. They are most known for their practice of building earth mounds. The earth mounds were pyramids with flat tops. Homes, temples, and other buildings were built on top of some mounds. Other mounds were used for burials, **ceremonies**, meetings, and more.

In time, people within the Mississippian Culture began dividing into groups. They built more and more communities. These groups became nations of people. The Muscogee were one of many that lived well in the area.

EARTH MOUNDS

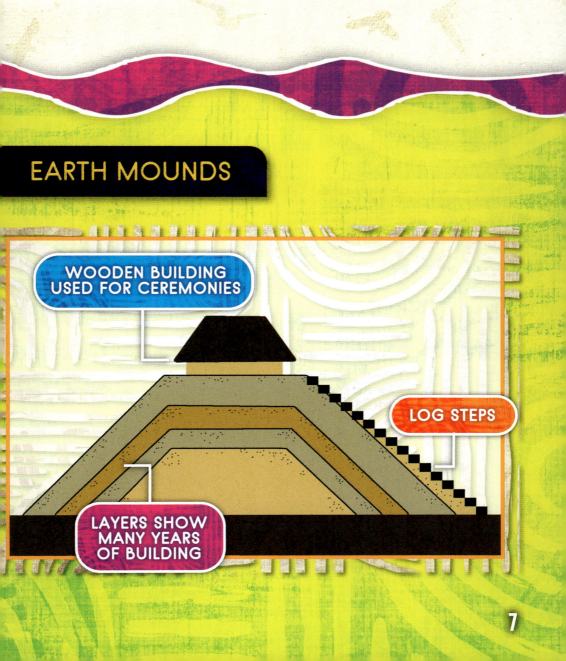

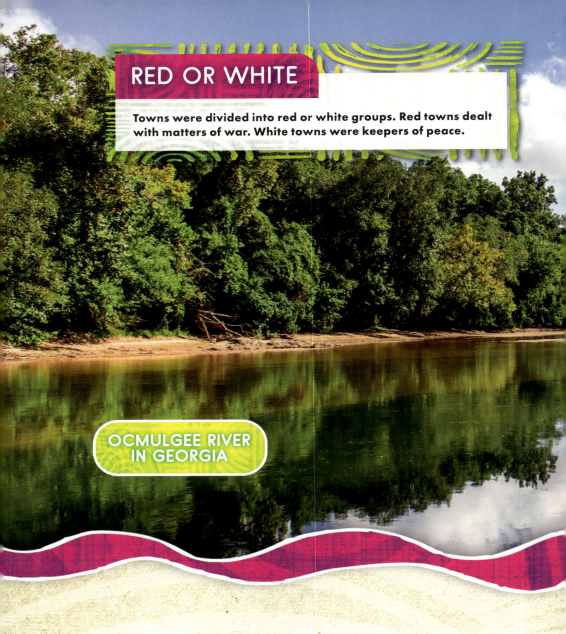

RED OR WHITE

Towns were divided into red or white groups. Red towns dealt with matters of war. White towns were keepers of peace.

OCMULGEE RIVER IN GEORGIA

Ancestral Muscogee developed a **confederacy** of tribes. They developed *talwas*, or towns, that expanded throughout the river valleys of today's Georgia and Alabama. Each town was governed independently by a *miko*, or town Chief.

ILLUSTRATION OF A TALWA

   Towns were often built around a town square with a **sacred** fire. This is where ceremonies took place. Homes were built around the square. They were often rectangular and made with poles covered in mud. Plant materials such as bark were used to make roofs. People planted gardens and fields beyond the towns.

Muscogee towns were made up of **clans**. Most clans had an animal name. People in the same clan tended to live near one another within the towns. The clans were **matrilineal**. Women were in charge of the household. When couples married, they built homes near the woman's family.

Ancestral Muscogee relied on farming, hunting, and gathering for food and goods. Women were responsible for farming. They grew corn, beans, and squash often. Men hunted deer, bears, squirrels, and turkeys. They also fished. Nuts and fruits were a big part of their diet, too.

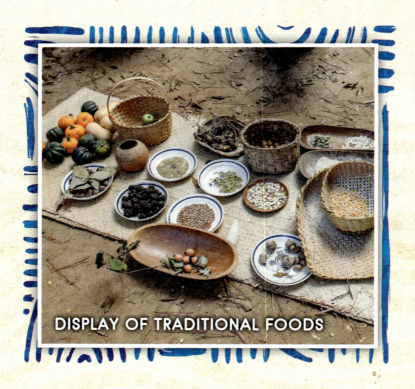

DISPLAY OF TRADITIONAL FOODS

THREE SISTERS

Corn, beans, and squash are known as the "Three Sisters." These three foods grow well together. They were important foods for many nations across today's U.S.

EUROPEAN CONTACT

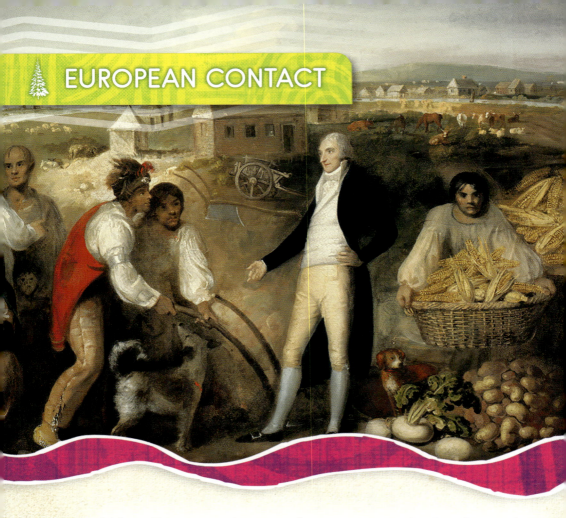

When Europeans began taking interest in the Southeast, the Muscogee were located in two areas. The English referred to them as the Upper Creeks and the Lower Creeks. The Upper Creeks continued to live a traditional lifestyle. The Lower Creeks were more influenced by the English.

Americans looked to live on Muscogee land after the **Revolutionary War**. The U.S. government pressured the Muscogee to leave. Some Muscogee wanted to fight for their land. Other Muscogee believed staying peaceful would be best. This led to the Creek Indian War in 1813. Soon, the U.S. military joined the war.

UPPER AND LOWER CREEKS

The Upper and Lower Creeks were made up of distinct groups. The Upper Creeks included the Coweta. The Lower Creeks included the Tallapoosa and the Abeika.

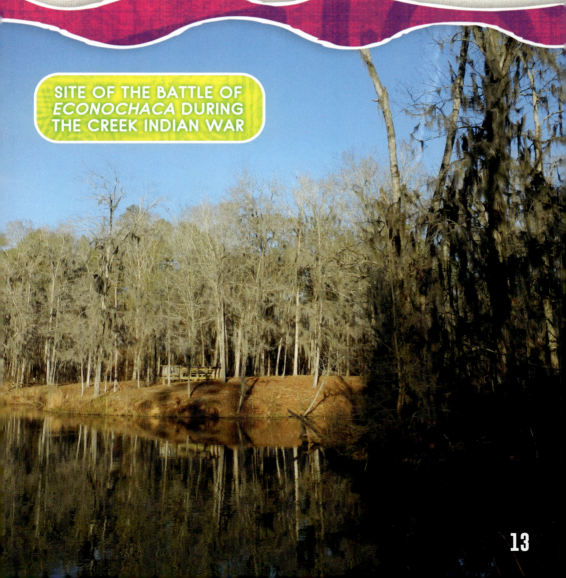

SITE OF THE BATTLE OF *ECONOCHACA* DURING THE CREEK INDIAN WAR

The war ended in 1814 at the Battle of *Cholocco Litabixbee*, or the Battle of Horseshoe Bend. Hundreds of Muscogee warriors died. The U.S. used the war to force all Muscogee to give up millions of acres of land. Most were forced west. Some Muscogee left to join the Seminoles.

Those who survived the forced removal worked to rebuild their lives. They established their government, built homes, and practiced their traditions. The U.S. put children in **boarding schools** to erase Muscogee **culture**. But the Muscogee fought to keep it alive.

FAMOUS MUSCOGEE

JOY HARJO

BIRTHDAY May 9, 1951

FAMOUS FOR
A writer and musician who became the first Native American Poet Laureate of the United States in 2019

14

SITE OF THE BATTLE OF *CHOLOCCO LITABIXBEE*

SEMINOLES

Many Native American peoples were forced from their homelands throughout the 1700s and 1800s. Some people from today's Georgia and Alabama moved to Florida for safety. Many of these people came together to become the Seminoles.

LIFE TODAY

Today, Muscogee people are members of various tribes located in Oklahoma, Alabama, Georgia, and Florida. Members live on **reservations** and in other places across the U.S. and the world. Some tribes are recognized by state governments. Others are recognized by the U.S. government. Two federally recognized tribes include the Muscogee Nation in Okmulgee, Oklahoma, and the Poarch Band of Creek Indians in Alabama.

The Muscogee Nation has over 100,000 members. It has a successful economy. It runs many casinos. The nation has hospitals and clinics. **Tourists** visit the reservation to learn about Muscogee culture. The College of the Muscogee Nation provides higher education to students.

16

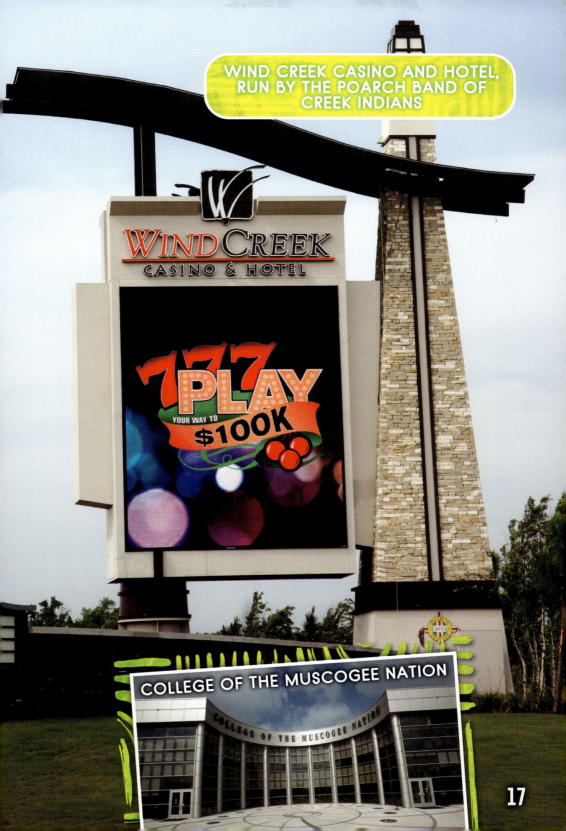

The Muscogee Nation's government works for its members. It has three branches that work together. The executive branch is led by the Principal Chief and Second Chief. The legislative branch has a 16-member **council** that makes laws and approves spending. The government also includes the Muscogee Nation District Court and the Supreme Court.

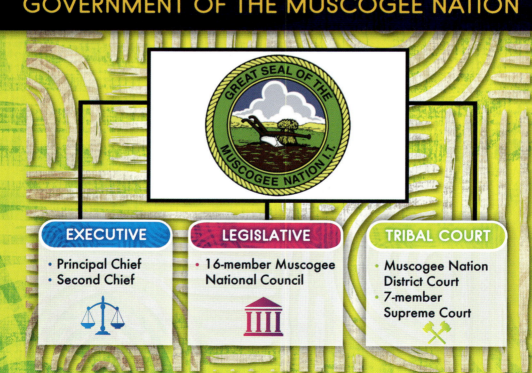

MUSCOGEE NATION GOVERNMENT BUILDING

MUSCOGEE NATION PRINCIPAL CHIEF DAVID HILL IN 2023

The government provides services to members. Childcare and education programs ensure children are cared for. Protective services help elderly members and those with disabilities. Recreation programs help members stay active.

CONTINUING TRADITIONS

MVSKOKE LANGUAGE PRESERVATION PROGRAM WEBSITE

There are many ways Muscogee people practice their culture today. One is through language. The Mvskoke Language **Preservation** Program helps keep the Mvskoke language alive. The program creates tools for language teachers. Interested members of the Muscogee Nation are welcome to learn the language of their ancestors.

The Mvskoke alphabet has 20 letters. It uses the same letters as English. Some letters sound similar to how they are said in English. Others have specific Mvskoke sounds.

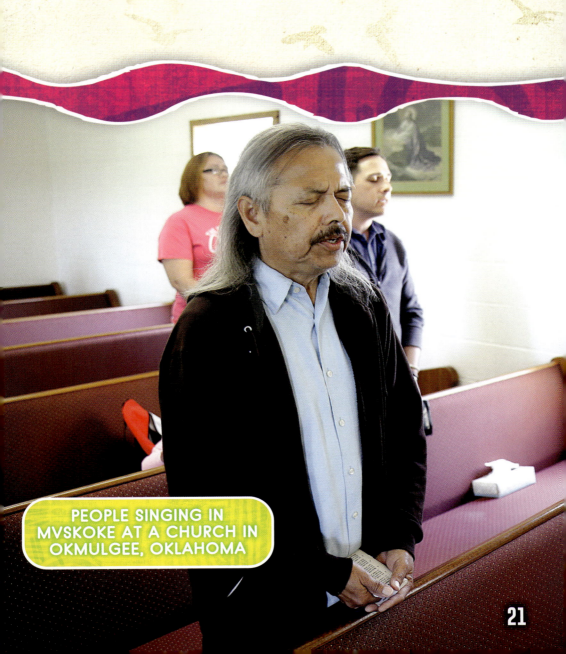

PEOPLE SINGING IN MVSKOKE AT A CHURCH IN OKMULGEE, OKLAHOMA

MUSCOGEE NATION COUNCIL HOUSE

MARY SMITH

The Muscogee Nation's Council House hosts classes that teach some traditional Muscogee practices. Some Muscogee people learn to make corn husk dolls and traditional baskets. Mary Smith is an award-winning basket weaver who teaches her students ancient methods of weaving. Ancestral Muscogee collected honeysuckle each fall for weaving. Today, round reeds from China are more commonly used.

The Muscogee Nation's Redstick **Gallery** supports Muscogee artists. Many artists use traditional methods and ideas to create their work. Visitors can view and buy original art including paintings, pottery, books, and jewelry.

TRADITIONAL CORN HUSK DOLLS

CORN HUSKS

SINEW

TRADITIONAL CORN HUSK DOLL

Muscogee people honor their ancestors for preserving traditions and culture. Each year, the Muscogee Nation comes together for the Council Oak Ceremony. It is held at the Creek Nation Council Oak Park in Tulsa, Oklahoma. Long ago, Muscogee brought ashes from fires in their homeland. Today, the Council Oak tree grows where they placed the ashes.

Songs are an important part of Muscogee ceremonies. Rattles made from female box turtle shells provide music during some ceremonies. Women wear the shells on the lower parts of their legs and stomp. Men sing while women create the beat.

RATTLES MADE FROM TURTLE SHELLS

STICKBALL

Stickball is one of the oldest sports in North America. It has been played by many Native American nations. In October 2022, members of the Eastern Band of Cherokee Indians, the Chickasaw Nation, the Mississippi Choctaw Nation, and the Muscogee Nation came together for a stickball tournament on traditional Muscogee land.

FIGHT TODAY, BRIGHT TOMORROW

BOARDING SCHOOL

Muscogee ancestors experienced many hardships throughout U.S. history. The use of boarding schools was one of them. Today, the Muscogee Nation works to honor survivors and descendants through the Remembrance Walk. People share stories, learn about the past, and make progress for the future.

Some Muscogee are working to make Ocmulgee Mounds into Ocmulgee National Park and Preserve. This sacred land in Georgia was once the center of the Muscogee Nation. If it becomes a national park, the Muscogee would manage it with the U.S. government. This would help protect the land and culture of the Muscogee!

OCMULGEE MOUNDS

TIMELINE

1836
Following the Indian Removal Act of 1830, thousands of Muscogee are forced from their homelands

AROUND 1540
Spanish explorer Hernando de Soto is the first European that the Muscogee encounter

1970
The U.S. government allows the Muscogee Nation to elect their own Principal Chief

1901
The Muscogee cooperate with Congress's Dawes Act which gives Muscogee people less control over land

1814
After the Creek Indian War, both Upper Creeks and Lower Creeks are forced to sign a treaty to give up millions of acres of land

1975

The Indian Self-Determination and Education Assistance Act gives Native American nations the right to take control of some services such as education

2004

The first classes begin at the College of the Muscogee Nation

1984

The U.S. government recognizes the Poarch Band of Creek Indians

2018

The Muscogee Nation opens the Okemah Community Hospital

1981

The Muscogee Nation begins allowing people with proof of their Muscogee ancestors to enroll as members

GLOSSARY

ancestral—related to relatives who lived long ago

boarding schools—schools created throughout the 1800s to remove traditional Native American ways of life and replace them with American culture

ceremonies—sets of actions performed in a particular way, often as part of religious worship

clans—groups of people who share a common ancestor

confederacy—a group of Native American nations

council—a group of people who meet to run a government

culture—the beliefs, arts, and ways of life in a place or society

descendants—people related to a person or group of people who lived at an earlier time

gallery—a place where art is on display

matrilineal—related to or based on following a family line through the mother

Mississippian Culture—the last major prehistoric culture of the southeastern river valleys of North America, lasting from about 700 CE to the arrival of the first European explorers

preservation—the act of keeping something in its original state

reservations—lands set aside by the U.S. government for the forced removal of Native American communities from their original lands

Revolutionary War—the war between 1775 and 1783 in which the United States fought for independence from Great Britain

sacred—relating to spiritual or religious practice

tourists—people who travel to visit another place

traditionally—related to customs, ideas, or beliefs handed down from one generation to the next

TO LEARN MORE

AT THE LIBRARY

Chuculate, Eddie. *This Indian Kid: A Native American Memoir.* New York, N.Y.: Scholastic Focus, 2023.

Perish, Patrick. *Alabama.* Minneapolis, Minn.: Bellwether Media, 2022.

Sexton, Colleen. *Oklahoma.* Minneapolis, Minn.: Bellwether Media, 2022.

ON THE WEB

FACTSURFER

Factsurfer.com gives you a safe, fun way to find more information.

1. Go to www.factsurfer.com.

2. Enter "the Muscogee" into the search box and click 🔍.

3. Select your book cover to see a list of related content.

INDEX

boarding schools, 14, 26
ceremonies, 6, 9, 24
Chief, 8, 18, 19
clans, 10
College of the Muscogee Nation, 16, 17
confederacy, 8
council, 18
Council House, 22
Council Oak Ceremony, 24
Creek Indian War, 12, 13, 14, 15
culture, 4, 8, 9, 10, 14, 16, 20, 22, 23, 24, 25, 27
earth mounds, 6, 7, 27
foods, 10, 11
future, 26, 27
government of the Muscogee Nation, 18, 19
Harjo, Joy, 14
history, 4, 6, 7, 12, 13, 14, 15, 19, 22, 25, 26
homeland, 4, 12, 14, 15, 24, 25, 27
housing, 9, 10
map, 4, 16
members, 16, 18, 19, 20, 25
Mississippian Culture, 6, 7
Muscogee Nation, 16, 17, 18, 19, 20, 22, 23, 24, 25, 26, 27
Mvskoke, 4, 5, 20, 21
Mvskoke Language Preservation Program, 20
name, 4, 12, 13
Ocmulgee Mounds, 27
Ocmulgee River, 6, 8
Poarch Band of Creek Indians, 16, 17
Redstick Gallery, 23
Remembrance Walk, 26
reservations, 16
Seminoles, 14, 15
Smith, Mary, 22
stickball, 25
timeline, 28–29
towns, 8, 9, 10
traditional corn husk dolls, 22, 23
traditions, 4, 6, 7, 8, 9, 10, 11, 12, 14, 20, 22, 23, 24, 25
U.S. government, 12, 14, 16, 27
warriors, 14